This book is meant to raise awareness about what is happening around us and meant to be a voice to those who have faced any of these challenges and issues at some point in their lives. This book is also dedicated to my one and only beloved Ezzeddine family who have always been there for me and supported me throughout my life and career choices. I want to give a huge thank you to my mother and father for encouraging me since a young age to write and to show my writings to the world. I want to also thank my friends Sarah Swaid, Zeina Yahfoufi, Christina Ismail Halabi and Ribal Yehia who have helped me edit, and design this book as well as the friends who know who they are that have supported me. Thank you.

The Clash in Mental Health and Illness

New Friend

Hi tinnitus, how are you today?
Are you going to annoy me?
Please don't be loud
I want to feel the silence today
The silence of a quiet room

Hi tinnitus, how are you today?
Are you going to be moody?
Please don't switch from a silent ocean
wave to an angry whistleblower
I want to bear you
To push your sound to my background noise

Hi tinnitus, how are you today?
Are you going to attack me with anxiety?
Please be good to me
I want to feel calm today
The tranquility of feeling relaxed

Hi tinnitus, how are you today?
Are you going to wake me up?
Please let me sleep
I want to dream deeply today
And wake up from a good night's sleep

Hi tinnitus, how are you today?
Are you going to be my friend?
Please let's be friends
I want to feel the friend in you

Hi tinnitus, I am ready for you today
I will be your friend if you decide to stay
But I will ignore you when you
decide to ruin my day

Hi tinnitus, I have accepted you today
So let's play a game
Why don't you play your rhythm all day?
While I sing along and sway
For there is nothing else I can do
But to find a friend in you

* **Note:** Tinnitus is an inner ear disorder
with ringing or noise coming
from the ears/brain

Through Sickness and in Health

I will love you
Blind, deaf or paralyzed
I will love you
How you may say?

When you're blind
I will create a world for you
I will take you places
To the sea, mountains and cities
I will describe every detail for you
How crystal clear and blue the sea is
How huge and snowy the mountains are
How old and colourful cities are
With their tall skyscrapers
And night view city lights

I will make you imagine it all
Just like reality
I will make you touch and feel
everything that is beautiful
So that you can see

When you're deaf
I will leave notes around and about
To remind you that I love you
I will write down how the music sounds
And act it out for you
I will dance with you until the sun rises
So you can feel the rhythm of the music
I will make you imagine what the
beauty of music sounds like

When you are paralyzed
I will carry you around
I will never let you miss out on life
To see and feel all that there is
To enjoy every moment
I will push you down the road to feel the
breeze and the beauty around you

For as long as your heart still beats
My love for life with you will beat too

Through sickness and in health
I will love you

A Devil on Earth

People say the devil is only in hell
But can't they see him in reality?
Not in wars and in people
But in our air and in diseases

Cancer is a devil
A devil killing millions
Every single day
Strangers and loved ones

It kills every inch of a person's body,
 mind and soul
Spreading and spreading like a plague
Doesn't want to stop
Always hungry for more

It is not enough to harm just the lungs
Cancer wants the brain too
The breasts, the bones, the ovaries
Everything to take a human's body away

What kind of disease is this?
What disease destroys a person like this?
What disease let's a person suffer?
Until they surrender and take their last breath?

This is not a disease
It is devil on earth
And he will not leave until he kills us all

Bird with Wings

I wish to be a bird with wings
That can fly
So high above the sky
A bird that loses its way
To just get lost

A bird that wanders
And admires the beauty of the earth
And watches over everyone

A bird that is free
Free from the human world
Free from the laws
Free from the dull routines
That humans are born to follow

I wish to be a bird
That knows and feels freedom
A bird that will look down
And see humans as machines
Living similar lives of responsibilities
And a bird that will just keep moving forward

With nothing to hold me back
Losing my way in-between the clouds
The rain and the snowy mountains
To places so far away
Where only a bird can reach and see
That is the true meaning of freedom
For humans are the ones living in a cage

The Clash of Misconceptions

False Conceptions

They think they know it all
When all they do is just sit on a phone call
Spreading false information and interpretation
That we don't have a nation
Mocking our Middle East
For our daily dinner feast

Shocked that all we have are camels
Yet they aren't aware that we have other mammals
And they wonder how do we survive
When all they see is a person holding a gun and a knife

They are convinced that we are uncivilized
With most of our citizens being criminalized
And this makes them feel sorry
But we should tell them not to worry

Instead they should come
Leave where they are from
See the Middle East with their own eyes
And ignore all believed lies

Once they leave here
They'll go back with a tear of joy
Telling others that the Middle East is not what you hear
The Mediterranean Sea is so blue and crystal clear

They'd be telling others
About the strong Arab mothers
And how Beirut is the small Paris
With people listening to Calvin Hariss

People so eastern yet western
And it is not an opinion
But a fact of the Lebanese union

And that is why people should expand their knowledge
Not just by graduating from college
But by traveling and marveling
At the variety of cultures
And their fascinating sculptures

They should explore and see more
Of the other world
A world so unknown to their nation
Because all that is known to them is
ignorance and discrimination

My Islam

The religion of peace and humanity
Simply condemns brutality
Nothing what the media says
About a Muslim that regularly prays

True, the Islamic terrorist group of ISIS
Has caused chaos and a crisis
All over the Middle East
Creating a fallacy that every Muslim is a beast

I see the world now fears Islam
The religion of our Prophet Muhammad and our Imam
That taught us about love and purity
Not about hate and cruelty

What these terrorists have done
Is accepted by none and I mean none
They do not represent my religion
Nor are they welcomed in my region

They have done nothing but abuse my Islam
And took away the “ahlam”
Meaning dreams of others
Such as children, men and mothers

They are left crying
Because they have witnessed their loved ones dying
In a brutal, horrible and immoral way
No religion in the name of history accepts this in a way
Religion is all about morals, peace and love
For reality is a temporary test
To see how we treat ourselves and the rest

Therefore, do not hate my religion
Hate the people who abuse it
And kill in the name of my Islam

For our Imam has taught us more than this
We Muslims are human beings
Just like Christians and Jews
So why do we have to take the blame?

The world needs to stop being ignorant and cynical
For not all Muslims are terrorists
So stop with the Anti-Muslim rallies
And let us be friends in your street alleys

My religion of peace
Is my Islam that you'll never know
Unless you read the Holy Quran
And understand the beauty of its words

Only then will you know who Allah is
He is the one of my Islam
And in the name of Allah
I pledge and swear on the Holy Quran
That we Muslims are not terrorists

The Clash in Love

To my Ex-lover

To my ex -lover,

It is never too late
To walk away
And while I walk away
I am lifting my head high
For I was a woman who loved deeply and truly

A woman who gave her all and would have went
across the world to be with you
A woman who did not give up

And a woman who did not want to lose hope
And the hardest thing I could do
Is to walk away from you still in love with you
But the hardest thing I could see
Is seeing you walk away knowing that
Without a single care

So today,
I am walking away
I am letting you go

Hoping life will show you what you have lost
What you could have done to make it work

And throughout life, you will be searching for
me in every woman you meet
And life will tell you that woman is a long -lost
memory that you failed to care for

A woman you were afraid of loving
A woman you just let go

But that woman is gone now
That woman is nowhere to be found
That woman is the woman you lost

Invisible

It's sad how you can become so
intimate with someone
Yet the next day
You become strangers that can't even say hello

You are not just a stranger
But you are invisible
He does not ask about you
But you want to ask about him
He knows nothing about you
And you want to know so much about him

But you have become invisible to him
While he is continuing his life
Like you never existed
You never talked

You never fell in love
And you never met
The whole time you were invisible

You observe his newsfeed
You watch his every move
But he could care less
About you and your new uploaded red dress
You are invisible

To him, you do not exist
You are a shadow
That has vanished from his life

And he cannot feel
The pain of being invisible
Because to you, he is there
He is visible

In Another World

This man in another world
Treats his woman like an emerald
He stares at her as if she was a shine
Whispering to himself "one day she will be mine"

To him she's like an angel
In love with her blonde curl
And to him she is precious
Cursing her love for being contagious

He loves her madly
But she does not know him sadly
He desires for a beautiful summer day
So he could watch her sway

His eyes start to tear
With drops so crystal clear
Wondering why doesn't she open her eyes
And begin to realize

A man who will die to see her smile
And who will walk that mile
Just to get a glimpse of her pretty face
Wearing that beautiful red lace

He imagines her as his wife
Hoping for the rest of his life
But she does not know his existence
Yet he continues his persistence

Some day he tends to believe
That he will overcome his grief
One day he tends to pray
That she will hear his say

Not today, but maybe some other day
For she knows a man like him
Does not exist
For he's only a mist

The Clash in Travel

Global citizen

Like a foreigner,
I desire to explore every corner
Climbing every mountain
And enjoying every fountain

Riding through rice fields in Bali
Yet admiring ancient fortresses in Mali
Wandering through Buddha temples
in Thailand
While bowing to the king of Swaziland

Glancing at the Taj Mahal in India
But dancing to a folk song in Serbia
Spinning tango style to Argentina
Walking like an empress to the Great wall of China

Sailing on the Nile river of Uganda
Reaching for the diamonds in the
capital of Angola, Luanda
Passing through Malawi's capital Lilongwe,
Glimpsing at the wildlife of Zimbabwe

Running through the kingdom of Jordan
in Amman
Fishing in the Arabian Peninsula of Yemen

Meditating in the beauty of nature
in Sri Lanka,
Standing on the lions horn in Cape town, South Africa

This is a foreigner walking on a traveler's
map of dreams

But..
Getting lost in the deserts of Oman
Finding a child in need in Sudan

Mourning the loss of those in Syria
Hating on rights being violated in Saudi Arabia

Watching the massacres of Central
African Republic
Hoping to bring justice to the public

Crying for those in hunger in Somalia
Wondering why is there so much
poverty in India?

Fighting for those forced into child
marriage in Pakistan
Trying to help them escape to Kazakhstan
Smuggling human basic needs in Iraq
Yet knowing if caught there's no
way coming back

Remembering the genocide of Armenia
Admitting the same happened in Bosnia

Stopping child labour in Sierra Leone
Wondering why can't they be left alone?

Lamenting the deaths of those in Liberia
Yet long back many were sentenced to
death in Siberia
Hoping one day peace would come to Palestine
And it will be set free as Liechtenstein

This is a foreigner walking on a traveler's
map of screams

Feeling hopeless, feeling helpless
And all I can do is be selfless
But people could care less
About the world's mess

Yes, Life is beautiful
And Life is bountiful

But no, reality is depressing
And it's just distressing

Therefore, how can I be a foreigner
walking on a travelers map of dreams
when all I hear in my dreams are screams?

The Clash in Social Inequality

Rio de Janeiro

When one thinks of Rio
He pictures the beautiful beach of Ipanema
He pictures the luxurious life of Copacabana
He fantasizes about the parties,
nightlife and human bodies
This is how one tends to perceive Rio

But when I think of Rio
I picture the other part of it
The part that shows the everyday reality
The reality I grew to learn and see
With my own mind and eyes

As I go to parties
I see the atmosphere of Brazilians
So full of life and joy
The way they know how to move to the
music and enjoy life
But at the same time
I see the beggar outside watching
And he too is dancing his life away

As I walk down the streets
I see the different lifestyles
The rich mansions and Middle-class houses
And right next to them
I see the favelas of the underprivileged

Both rich and poor living right next
to each other But you see them living
in completely different realities

As I enter a favela
I come across beautiful joyful faces
People so friendly and welcoming
People that live through violence everyday
But they still survive
I once read on a wall of a favela
"The rich want peace to continue being rich,
 we want peace to continue living"
What a powerful message indeed

As I meet people
I don't understand why so many
Are afraid of favelas and its people
They talk about them as if they're criminals
When they are not

The artists, dancers, and musicians
The ones you shouldn't be afraid of
The ones you should befriend and learn from
The same way I learnt from them

As I worked with them
I ended up loving them
Being inspired by them
For all what they have been through
They still manage to put on a smile and survive

Rio de Janeiro
You are a city full of emotions
I hated you and loved you
You've made me cry
You've made me smile
You've made me understand
You've made me see the truth
And I'll carry the truth with me

To all the homeless people
To all the favela people
You are not alone
People like me do care
And will forever care
Till we meet again Rio

The Clash of Dreams

She was Here

Waking up every day knowing
that it is a bright new day
To make a difference, to make a change
To leave a memory engraved
somewhere in the park
Or maybe on someone who's left in the dark

Leaving my footprints and memories everywhere
Making them wonder who is this
woman coming into my life out of nowhere?
This woman that comes and spreads a positive aurora
And suddenly disappears all the way to Bora Bora

This woman makes people miss her presence
And can't bear her absence
A woman people crave for her company
As they wave goodbye to her from their balcony

A woman like a free bird
that flies away to places
Exploring the crystal ice glace and a green natural space
Yet like a messenger
Telling people not to feel any lesser

In every country, I step foot on
I want the little homeless boy to know
That he is like my son
I want the abused girl to know that
She is like a pearl
I want those facing an issue
To know that I am their tissue
And their ear and forever loyal peer

I want to leave a memory in a place, on someone
And when I am long gone
They will remember me
Even when I am across the sea
And they will smile
When they see me coming from a mile

Whispering to themselves “she is here”
To amend the crack in our hearts
That the world has torn apart
And even though we cried
Because of her we survived

I want to touch lives,=
Spread a positive vibe and spirit
Leaving memories like a manuscript
So people will remember I was there
Coming out of nowhere
Spreading my endless love and care
To those in despair

And in every country, I’ve stepped on
I have not only left my footprints
But my own human prints
On people that I have come to love
And people that have come to love me back
And that is why I am always ready to pack
To go somewhere and leave a mark there
And hear people whispering she was here

"He"

**To my Nepali friend who taught me
the meaning of a simple life with dreams**

He wasn't an ordinary human
He was Nepali yet he looked so Cuban
And all he aimed for was to strive
For he wasn't born for normal life

He may be young
But he has the mind of a wise man
A young lad full of dreams and ambitions
Creating network of telecommunications
For the people of his beloved Nepal

He don't need no money
Only a simple house and a honey
In the land of his home
But he also yearns to visit Rome

His mind is following the map
Yet he believes he's in a trap
But his mind is already going places
Creating ideas for empty
Sites, restaurants, stores and stations
With hands that can build a house out of crystallization

What an extraordinary human he is
That wasn't born for normal life
With a smart mind and a kind heart
And this kind of man is never poor
Rich with the love of people around him
Rich in his soul

This kind of man
Will be going places
Not only his mind but he, himself
Will be going everywhere
Leaving his footprints
And telling you "I was there"

The Clash of being an Arab Woman

Freedom

So why freedom?
It's mainstream they say
But let me explain,

I was born a woman
An Arab woman from the Middle East
Which makes me a minority
Living under a patriarchy

A system of men power and dominance
Where women are expected to be submissive
Expected to cook, clean and obey
With no dreams and aspirations

A woman with aspirations is considered rebellious
And not desirable for marriage
But this woman could care less
All she wants is freedom

She was born believing in freedom
The freedom to be herself
The freedom to do what she loves
The freedom to live, learn, travel and experience

The freedom to be a free woman
In a men's only world
That expects her to obey and sit

And that is why I desire to carve a tattoo
In my mother tongue saying freedom
Because freedom is what i fight for
It is what my ears hear
And what my eyes seek
For as long as I am a woman
Living as a minority under the power of the majority

I am an Arab Woman

I am a woman, an Arab woman
And you can hear my footsteps comin'
It may seem intimidating
But it is rather fascinating

I am an Arab woman
And my beauty shall not be exposed
to any undeserving man
As I walk away and sway
They too follow me the same way

An Arab woman
That they try to get a glimpse of
For I am a woman with hidden secrets
With a certain beauty
For I am a woman of the Middle East
A woman born and raised with purity

I am an Arab woman
In the land where my great grandfathers have fought

While seeing their women being bought
Through bloody never-ending wars
And have endured ample sores

I am an Arab woman
In the land of the Middle East
Where my great grandmothers have endured the pain
Of losing loved ones such as====
fathers and brothers
And their ashes are what only remain

I am an Arab woman
Born as a rebel
Watching every missile
Explode in front of my eyes
And all is left are cries
Of children, men and women

I am an Arab woman
Born with strength
Like my great grandmothers had
until they took their last breath
Revolution and freedom
Is what I desire and admire

I am an Arab woman
A woman of the Middle East
That is fearless of every beast
For every bomb and explosion
Only makes us stronger not with anger
But with a passion to fight
For what we believe is right

I am an Arab woman
That carries the Middle East on

my head and shoulders
As i walk and notice wanderers
Trying to get a glimpse of the
woman behind the veil

I am an Arab woman
With pain and tears in my eyes
For the distress of explosions in one eye
And happiness and joy in another eye
For i am a woman of contrasting emotions

I am a woman, an Arab woman
A woman that does not confide her pride
And you can hear my footsteps comin'

Them Versus Me

They tell me
You are just a woman
Not any woman but an Arab woman

They tell me
You are not just an Arab but a Lebanese woman
But not just an Arab Lebanese woman
But also, a Muslim woman
And that is simply the reason why
Your voice will never be heard
And you are destined to failure

But I tell them
Yes, I am an Arab woman
But I was born a rebel
For I have the eyes and mind of a revolution
And that is simply the reason why
I am destined to greatness and success

The Clash of loving those from other Cultures, Religions and Distance

Foreign Love

On the continent of the Americas
I came from the Middle East
And he came from the Far East
With different cultures and religions
Different humans attracted to one another

For all the ups and downs we had
We always overcame them
For all the times, we pushed each other away
We always pulled each other back
And that to me was a strong connection

Distance may separate us physically
But our hearts, minds and souls
are still connected
And these will overcome the distance
If we want to fight for it

But I know as soon as he sets foot on that
plane back home
I will just be memory like this foreign
land that connected us

A memory that reminds us of the chances
that we failed to take
A memory of what we could have been
A memory engraved behind our minds
A memory reminding us that we could have

said "forgive me, I am imperfect"
And accept one another as we are
If you had let me love you and
let yourself to love me

But I can only wonder as I start to miss him
and watch him get on that
Plane across the world
Will he ever meet me halfway?

Too Different

I can't be with you, he said
Why?
Because of our different religions

I can't be with you, he said again
Why?
Because of our different cultures

I can't be with you, he kept saying
Why?
Because of the distance between
us in our two different countries

I can't be with you, he finally said
Why?
We are just too different

Why can't you try I said
At least compromise?
I told you I can't he said
We are not meant to be

We are not meant to be in your world I said
But in my world,
We can be two different lovers
In our traditional wedding gowns with a
mix of different rituals
African drums with the Middle Eastern
Dabke to the Asian traditional dance

We can be two different lovers

While I pray on my Islamic praying mat
And while you pray to your Buddha God
Or to Jesus on a Palm Sunday

We can be two different lovers
With beautiful mixed race children
Growing up already open to different
 religions and cultures
Speaking at least 3 different languages
How educated would they be?

To me, a life and family with
differences is a blessing
It is a the reflection of our
globalized world of diversity

That our societies are failing to accept
We are the reflection of what
 they are afraid of
For co-existence, love and diversity
Are a threat to our world

We will be an example, a voice challenging
What our societies were born to hate

The Clash in Parenthood

How are you a Mother?

I am a mother you say,
But how can you be a Mother when you
have no love for your children?

Do you even know what a mother is?
A mother lives for her children
A mother gives her soul to her children

So tell me how are you a mother?
When you give no love, and no attention
to those you gave life to?

How can you be a mother?
When you only love yourself?
When your son is standing there
With tears in his eyes
And you feel nothing?

You ignore his emotions, his presence
And you still believe you are a mother?

Your son asks you for a penny
And you refuse
He is left alone and broke
You were his only hope of love
His only home

His father has abandoned him
And now his mother too?
So tell me, how are you a mother
When you abandon your children?

They grow old without a mother's love
They grow not knowing what it
feels like to have a mother
To love and comfort them
And to protect them from this
terrifying world

How can a mother be so cruel?

The Clash in the Refugee crisis in times of war

I am Sorry

To the Syrian child
I am sorry
You lost your mother
I am sorry
You lost your father
And your brother and sister

To the Syrian mother
I am sorry
You lost your child and children
I am sorry
You lost your husband
Your life partner

To the Syrian father
I am sorry
You lost your family
I am sorry
You lost your life
Where you were someone
And had a voice

To the Syrian family
I am sorry
You lost your roots
Your land and your home
I am sorry
You lost your world

To the Syrian refugees
I am sorry
You all had to flee from your country
And settle for less
In our countries

I am sorry
You are left with no voice
In our countries
I am sorry
Your future is not clear

I am sorry
You are being mistreated
I am sorry
For all the racist, discriminatory remarks
You have heard

I am sorry
For the physical and verbal abuse
You've encountered and endured
I am sorry
For the poor living conditions

I am sorry
Your children have to work
At a young age to help you

But most of all
To Syria,
I am sorry
That my sorry
Does not make up for what the
 world has done to you

I am sorry
That my sorry
Will not bring back your loved ones
Nor your homes
It is just a sorry from us humans
That feel with you
But are powerless
In a cruel world
Full of hate and wars
The greed to destroy
For selfish interests

Forgive me Syria
For what the world has done to you
All i can do as a powerless human
Is to say i am sorry

Million Voices

Can you hear the million voices?
Of the cries of the children
Registered as refugees?
Can you feel their pain?
Especially when a dollar is what they only gain?

They stand and watch and stare
At those that are not willing to spare
Not a single smile nor a hand
Because all they care about is a
fashion luxurious brand
That child in need sees their greed
Yet he chooses to forget
For he knows such people would
treat him like a pet

These people tend to live in their fantasy
Feeling the joy and ecstasy
While neglecting the truth of reality
And it's never ending brutality

They carry on with their lives
While others are being killed with sharp knives
And they be saying "well life is unfair"
But the truth is that they don't really care

Those kids have lost fathers and mothers
As well as so many others
Imagine seeing a loved one
Gone right in front of your eyes
Your cry then would be one
of the children's cries

It is provoking to see those choking
Their lives being taken away
in a blink of an eye
And the last sound you hear
is their cry

One may be innocent and cause no harm
Yet when you look close he has a bruised arm
And you'd be asking yourself why?
Later on, he's taken away
and you'd be saying goodbye

You no longer see that man
You no longer see that woman
You no longer see that child
For they are gone to a better place
Away from the world of disgrace

But can you hear the other million
voices of those still living?

The Clash of a Woman's Body

Sacred Body

They preach for gender equality
Women and men are equal,
But born different

When men look at a woman
They see a beautiful living creature
They admire her from head to toe
Paying close attention to her face and body

Yet some tend to abuse this beautiful creature
Rather than caress her gently
They become rough and harm her painfully

These fools don't see the beauty
and importance of a woman
They only see their frustrations
and lust of suppressed desires

But what they don't know
Is that a woman's body is sacred?
It is divine, a valuable jewel
To be found and to be kept safe
To be loved and treasured

A woman's body comes in
all shapes and colours
A variety of different beauties everywhere
A woman's body is a masterpiece of Art

And men were born from a woman's body
Create their children from her body
Find their pleasure, satisfaction
and affection from her body
And they still ask why her body is sacred?

How can a man destroy a
beautiful piece of art?
How can he harm a sacred body?

Doesn't he know that a woman is a living goddess?
Given to a man like a holy religion book
To be cherished and embraced

For a woman's body is the one
who gives man life

Can't You See?

Don't get close to me
I will push you
Can't you see?
I am not a toy or your playboy
But a beautiful living creature

Don't kiss me
I will hurt you
Can't you see?
I am not made for a game
But a woman that doesn't take the blame
And has no shame

Don't touch me
I will bite you
Can't you see?
I am not just a body
But a human that is somebody

Don't look at me
I will blind you
Can't you see?
I am not an object
But a woman that deserves respect

And most of all don't love me
I will destroy you
Can't you see?
I am a woman that wants a man
To love my soul, mind, and heart
Not my body, face and legs apart

The Clash in Everyday Life

This is Life

I have walked by the streets
I have seen people begging for money

I have walked by the restaurants
I have seen people begging for food

I have walked by the schools
I have seen people begging for education

I have walked by the houses
I have seen people begging for a family

I have walked around the world
I have seen the poor
I have seen the hungry
I have seen the uneducated
I have seen the orphan
I have walked by the streets
I have seen people throw money

I have walked by the restaurants
I have seen people throw food

I have walked by the schools
I have seen people throw education

I have walked by the houses
I have seen people throw their family

I have walked around the world
I have seen the rich
I have seen the greedy
I have seen the foolish
I have seen the unthankful

The Clash of Humanity

A World of Disgrace

We humans were born innocent
Yet we have become so maleficent
We were born as people so wonderful
Yet we have become so fearful

The humans of today from different parts
Have become the ones of loveless hearts
So heartless with no mercy
Praising beliefs of hypocrisy

Religion and ethics both simply condemn
The cruelty and atrocities created by these men
Even before the existence
of civilization in Jerusalem

Its repulsive to admit
That the devils on earth
Are not willing to quit
Even if it meant killing a child at birth

Believe it or not
A Girl below 13 is forced to tie the knot
Treated as a sex slave
And if she is to misbehave
She is then shot

Believe that there are men
Crucifying humans as young as children
In the 21st century
And all you see is their cemetery

Humans have become so cruel
Bombing innocent young ones in a school
The world has become hell on earth
And women now fear birth

For their children
Will live among men
So heartless and fearless
Depriving them from their rights
Because all they'll know
Are sleepless nights

These children become fearful
Of the people of the universe
That Are no longer wonderful
These children are living in a world of a curse

I see humans but no humanity
Is a saying that applies
To the everyday cries
Of the never ending brutality
Caused by the human race
In a world of disgrace

Forgotten Promises

Forgotten promises
When what we had were compromises

During an escalating crisis
People prefer to be bias

They become deaf to the cries
While staring at the grey skies

Avoiding the devastating reality
Denying the truth of mortality

Watching the child in starvation
Beg in frustration

Seeing the child in thirst
Watching them drink first
He feels their apathy
And no sense of empathy

They simply lack humanity
And this is simply insanity

Insanity of the heartless
That have become so careless

In a world so materialistic
With people as fake as plastic

What have we become?
For the good are just some

Forgotten promises
Has become the new motto
When aid workers leave the premises

Forgotten promises
Has become the new greed
When the rich don't care if you bleed

All that we have become
Is a reflection of our forgotten promises

Dear Youth of Dreams

Dear Map of Dreams,
I woke up today feeling sad
And I think I am going mad
I keep spinning my globe
And my heart aches everywhere
Can you imagine all those lives gone?
Who would have thought
such tragedies would happen?

My dear youth of dreams,
The whole world is suffering
and facing pain
The whole world is aching
The clouds are gloomy
While they empty out their tears through the rain
For the world

They are crying for humanity
For all the innocent lives of men,women and children lost
For all the lands destroyed and taken away
For all the pain and sorrow we
humans have inflicted and endured

My dear youth of dreams,
Pray for humanity, for your
brothers and sisters
From all different races,
religions, and cultures

Pray for the world that you want to hold
And light up 203 candles instead of 1
For they are all suffering
For we are one nation in a world
that is hurting everyday

The Clash in Africa

Mama Africa

From Liberia to Nigeria
The king of the jungle walks arrogantly past his men
Who stand as still statues summoning an amen

From Zimbabwe to Malawi
The Africans dance till the shimmering sun rises
Despite their mournful political crisis

From Mozambique to Sierra Leone
The African kneel to their masters
Covering their aching
wounds with ample plasters

From Rwanda to Botswana
Where the petulance of the beggars never ends
There remains no difficulty in finding one that mends

From Djibouti to Burundi
Racism harbors distress
As honour and vengeance stand before
their spiteful heiress

From the tiny huts scattered at the
tip of this nation to the depths
of its own Sahara,
Africans chant what their souls
may recall "Hakuna matata hakuna matata"

**Note: hakuna matata is a swahili saying
that means "no worries for
the rest of our days"**

Key to Africa

I have no plan for Africa he said
I told him "you never know"
He argued "I do know, Africa is not for me"

A month later, Africa was calling him
Africa awaits you my dear friend
With its arms wide open

So let me tell you about Africa
There is no sunshine brighter
 than the African sun
No smiles wider than the African smiles

Take a peak outside your window
And see the wildlife like no other
Only in Africa

Only in Africa do you see the king
of the jungle among his prey
Drums, beads, sticks and stones
The simplest way of music

Once you hear the drums and the
marimbas playing
Your soul and body uncontrollably start to move

Walk around the streets of Africa
And you will see the vibrant colours
of their clothing designs

With women walking with their babies
wrapped around their backs
And pots with fruits and vegetables
on top of their heads

Learn about the history of Africa
And you will realize how rich
Africa was and still is
Most of its unity, land and
resources were stolen and shattered
By the greed of colonizers and invaders

When you look at Europe,please know that they became
partly rich because of Africa

Africa is rich, it is the future of the world
Maybe not today, but soon you will see
It is the mother of the world

A fascinating continent
With a variety of languages,
cultures and religions
A continent welcoming to all
A continent full of love and joy

That is my Africa

Go to Africa, stand on top of a rock
And watch the dark red sunset over
the never-ending land of its inhabitants
And its wild animals

Only then will you understand
my love for Africa
And the reason we met is for
me to be your key to Africa

So go now, Africa is calling you

The Clash in Staying Young

Forever Young

Waking up in the mangwanani (morning)
Feeling okay, feeling nani (better)
From a dream of old age
Yet I choose to strive

Staring at the beauty of nature
Admiring the colorful creature
Such as the age of youth
And yes it's the truth

Singing "tum hi ho" (you are the one)
You are the one in charge of your life oh
Young and beautiful I am
Strangers saluting yes ma'am

They say ashes to dust
I say dying is not a must
So come with me mon amie (my friend)
Let's explore la vie (life)

Tomorrow no sorrow

Let's kufamba (go walk)
And let's dance to the Brazilian samba

Let's sing life is loco (crazy)
So give me your ruoko (hand)

And let's sing to every man
Tum pagel ya ragel (You crazy man)
Sincerely a young woman

Wake up every day and don't rara (lie down)
All day my friend, just fara (happy)

The Clash of Losing Someone

I See You in Liberia

To my late Uncle Nabil,

Growing up and hearing Liberia
Your name always came to mind
I imagined Liberia as you

As I wonder about the joyful
smiles of the Liberian people
I can clearly see yours in them

As I picture the lively scenery
of nature in Liberia
I can feel the energy of life
you had coming alive

As I watch the Liberian people dancing
I smile and recall your dance moves
And I can feel you dancing among them

As I listen to the beat of the African drums
Your comforting voice sings to me again
Even the chaos of Monrovia city
Resembles the dark times that you faced

Even in the memory of wars of Liberia
I can remember you battling the war of cancer

Liberia cried for you, we cried for you
We are all lost without you
For the king of Liberia that you are
Has left a legacy on mother earth

Your name engraved in our hearts
As morning birds sing for you
And as people crave for your presence
You will be remembered every day

You are Liberia,
You are us,

Your beautiful soul keeps on living
For a legend like you never dies
I will see you in my heart, mind
And for sure I will see you in Liberia
Till we meet again

The Clash of Enemies

Not Your Duty

You think it's your duty to judge me
But this is my life
And I want you to let me be

But you tend to criticize
Rather than sympathize
And you believe others are inferior
While you're simply superior

You'd tell me I'm not good enough
But I'd reply with a "cough, cough"
And you aim to lower my self esteem
Just to enjoy seeing me scream

You may be heartless
But I am happy being selfless
And I hope you do not mind
That I tend to be kind

Even to those not worth it
And do not deserve any bit
But I have come to learn in life
That some carry a knife
To stab and hurt others
While staring at their crying mothers

But I knew it was you, you little cult
Stop pretending it wasn't your fault

You say you wish me success
But I know you want to see me in a mess
And when I fail
You begin to blackmail

You'd tell me I'm mentally sick
But it is your heart that is as thick as a brick
Wishing others no good
And manipulating those in your hood

Revenge is your sweetest joy
Even when you seemed so coy
You heartless human creature
Why were you born into this mother nature?

The Clash of Identity

Who are you?

When asked what is your religion?
I would say my religion is kindness
A religion of moral ethics and values

I would say I am a Muslim, and a Christian
I am also a Buddha, Jew and a Hindu
Therefore, I am all religions

Just like any religion
I believe in something powerful and
superior which is one God
And the only difference is that he
Has a different name in every religion
Yet he is still the one and only God

Just like Atheists,
I admire and believe in science and evolution
Therefore, just like everyone I am a human being

When asked what is your nationality?
I would say ask me where I am a local instead
For I am a global citizen of the world

I am a local in Beirut, Harare, Banjul, San Jose and Bangk
I have also felt like a local in New Delhi, and Rio de Janeir
Since these cities have touched my heart in many ways
But if you mean origin wise
Yes, I am Lebanese
But heart wise, I am Zimbabwean
Yet mentally and personality wise
I am a human being that believes in humanity

My nationality is a mixture of different nationalities
I am a little bit of everything
I am a human being

When asked what is your race?
I would say I am a mix
From the outside, I am white
From the inside, I am African and Arab
Therefore, I come different racial backgrounds
I am a human being

We can have the same nationality, religion and race
Yet we can be completely two different human beings

I may be kind yet you may be cruel
I may love to help, yet you may love to harm
I may stand up against racism, yet you are
the racist fool that I am standing up against

Therefore, let me answer your question
I am a human being just like yourself
And everyone else around you

And when asked what…
I would stop and say ask who…
Ask who are you rather than what are you
For if you ask me who am I?
I would tell you I am a mix of everything
I am a citizen in a world of diversity
with humans just like you

In a World full of Nationalities

The Lebanese refuse to
acknowledge their motherland,
Where they used to fight hand in hand

A majority of them live abroad,
Showing pride with their green card

Arrogant with their foreign passport,
As they enter the Lebanese airport

Walking around haughtily,
Hello, I'm from America,
And my name is Moe

But silly, they can tell your
Lebanese from your name
It's not like its John Daniel Macmaine
And I'm sure your real name
is Mohammad Hussein Ali
But you live to brag, and that's just sad

Being born overseas, over there,
Doesn't mean you should lack care,
This is your homeland, this is your blood

How come we never hear Americans and
Canadians say that they're Caribbean or Bulgarian?

I'll tell you why, it's because they're true patriots,
Regardless of the wars and riots

Why shouldn't we as Lebanese feel so?
You say you're from Moscow,
Since you were born in Russia,
But over there, Arabs are under pressure

You say you were born in Japan,
Therefore, you come from Tokyo
But that doesn't mean your Japanese
Because whether you like it or not,
you're actually pure Lebanese

Some tend to say "I'm from England
And my brothers from Scotland
Yet my mother is from Siberia
But my dad is from Liberia"

As said above, due to their limited mentality
Did that show a true display of one nationality?

No, it didn't,
You're just a foreign immigrant
Trying to act out and imitate what
you idealize of a stranger's state

Their passport, you plan to steal
But your true identity, you can't conceal

What makes you desire to be part of them?
When all they care about is their ego system

During a war, your beloved foreigners
are the first to run away and leave you behind,

They become selfish,
They don't really care
Yet you still try to be one of them
Neglect our despised government
Every government has its bad deeds.
So no comment, it's the same overseas

A passport is nothing, it has an expiration date
But your blood nationality doesn't

Be proud of it and forget it's frustrating
electricity problems, government issues,
social classes and obnoxious people
Those don't matter, it's simply reality

Therefore, don't let there be reasons
for you to be ashamed of your
homeland and act superior to your
people just because u desire
to be a foreigner

For those who haven't set
foot in their homeland,

Seek your origins,
And acknowledge the nation
Where people bleed the same
And cry the same tears

The Clash in Discrimination

Behind Beautiful Walls

In the Southeast subcontinent of India,
One walks in the streets of Delhi,
Until he comes across these beautiful walls

They aren't walls of a Raj Palace
But walls of a slum
Not any slum but the slum
of the less fortunate,

And behind these walls are
What the Indians call The Broken people

One may wonder why called as such?

The truth of these broken people
Born into the Hindu caste system
Discriminated and hated,
Deprived from their rights
as normal human beings

Marginalized as the untouchables
As one enters those walls
He doesn't see the untouchables

Nor does he see the broken people
But what he sees are the beautiful people

People with hearts so pure as gold
Poor yet rich with happiness,
Smiles that could light up your world
Eyes that could tell stories
Hands that could make peace within oneself

One may stare through the eyes of a child,
One may touch the skin of this child
Yet the child screams in fear
Thinking how could someone touch
an untouchable like me?

No, these are not the broken people
No, these are not the untouchables
And no, they are not the untouchables
because they'll touch your heart
Once you have touched theirs

They may be someone's broken people
yet to others like myself,
they are beautiful people

The Clash in Beirut

A Nation Yet to Unite

In a fractionalized state,
Where some from different religions
Avoid being your mate
Leaving Lebanon diffused
And everyone confused

One used to feel like a pigeon
That could fly away from religion
But today, one fears theocracy
From those willing to dismantle democracy

In the name of religion they say
Causing the land to decay
My beautiful Beirut
With different sects in dispute

Not knowing how to agree
Spinning heads 180 degree
They be pointing the finger
On whom to pull the trigger

These are the elites of Beirut
And they should be put on mute

They can run and they can hide
But they certainly can't confide
From the sorrow of reality
Due to their infidelity

They'd say they'd kiss this land and its mud
Yet their faces are printed with blood
Of the names of those who
 had their last breath
And were young and weren't expecting death

The success of their wealth
Comes out of filth
Due to their stealth from those in need
And this shows how there's so much greed

Even though my city
Is left to be in scarcity
My beloved city
Will never need pity

For one day
This land this soil
Will overcome its turmoil

The people shall rise and unite
Not just the sect of the Maronite
But the whole nation
Protesting against sectarianism
 and discrimination

They'd be chanting "We are one"
And an end to sectarianism has to be done
Side by side the nation's men
Will be praying Amen

The Clash of being a Foreign Migrant

Modern Slavery

Slavery is abolished they say
But why don't you come to the Middle East
Where Modern slavery still exists
and you can see the foreign=
Migrants raising their fists

They come from faraway lands
and end up with blood on their hands
They wanted to seek a better life
yet they were stabbed in the back with a knife

Madame is what they're forced to say
Can I have a piece of this
left over food if I may?
And where are their passports?
That were taken away ever since they came from the airport

They want to leave yet they're stuck in grief
Their families back home worried in disbelief
Wondering where are our daughters?
When all they hear is two per week
are victims of slaughters

Screaming for their freedom, and rights
When they are only welcomed with daily fights
The domestic migrant
workers most young at age
Have been living a life in a cage

Contracts ended,
salaries are non-existent
While work days off and
 days out are not persistent
Starved, tortured and beaten
A full day and they have not eaten

Slavery is abolished they say
But why don't you come to the Middle East
Where Modern slavery still exists
and you can see the foreign
migrants raising their fists

*__Note:__ that this is a generalization
and many families treat
their house helpers as members
of the family and this was
written to convey the struggles that they
face in a continent full of racism

The Clash in fighting for Human Rights

Kill Me

Woke up to news of abuse
And human rights violations
Watching people on the streets
preaching for justice
Activists, artists and victims

Holding slogans against
violence and corruption
Voicing their anger
through the megaphones
Then all of a sudden, gun shots
are heard from afar
Boom, the crowd dispersed

They shot the activist
who was the most visible
The one whose face was all over the media
The one who initiated it all
The one who called for an
end to human discrimination

Next day, people are mourning
And nothing is changing
We are back to zero
So what next?

Should we continue and risk our lives?
Or should we just stop
and protect ourselves?
Can we really change the world?
These questions roam
around my head every day

I was born to be a rebel,
a fighter, a voice
But standing out there seen
as the system's enemy
Can only get me arrested for
life or killed for good
I crawl back into my bubble
and just watch from a distance

The next day, another abuse,
another violation of human rights
No, I can't sit and just watch

I have to do something, say something
Take action and spread the message

To be silent and to do nothing,
won't change a thing
To be loud and to take action
won't change a thing
But how can we know if we don't try?
So I voice my anger against
the enemies of humanity

And I tell them, kill me as you please
As long as I am alive,
walking on my two feet
I will use this voice of mine

You can kill me, I am just one
But my voice can kill a whole society
And behind me stands a crowd of
thousands of other voices
Just like mine

Their voices stronger than your gun
For our voices represent a never
ending nation of activists
Standing in your faces against injustice
and human rights violations
So be my guest, and kill me if you please

My crowd of voices are waiting to be next

The Clash of Living in Poverty

Children of the Sun

So many children running around barefoot
Torn clothes, mud stains on their skins
And visible bony ribs sticking out
All I can see is poverty and hunger

So many children with tears in their eyes
Crying out of thirst for clean water
Worms in their bodies and infections all over
All I can see is the lack of health
care and water sanitation

So many children with curious minds
Yearning to study and learn
Books and pens out of their reach
All I can see is those who
cannot afford an education

So many children with no parents
Abandoned and orphaned
Yet spreading love to everyone they meet

All I can see are hearts full
of positive emotions

So many children with hearts like gold
Unconditionally giving and sharing
Wanting to smile and laugh out loud
All I can see are those who are happy to be alive

So many children who are underprivileged
With little than what we have
Yet running around with joy
Under the African heat

When I look at them
My heart breaks and my tears cannot stop
When they look at me
They stop and stare with faces
shining like a light of hope
For they are the children of the sun

The Clash of being an Immigrant away from Beirut

My Beirut

What is Beirut to you they may ask? Let me explain I say

Beirut to me is the Beirut that I imagine and long for when I am abroad. We all have the love-hate relationship with Beirut and its flaws, charms and mysteries. But Beirut to me is the city I miss when I am far away. While walking around the streets of San Jose in Costa Rica or the streets of Bangkok in Thailand, I stumble upon a Lebanese restaurant and I am overjoyed with excitement. I quickly enter the restaurant to smell the beauty of my Lebanese food again and to see the walls full of pictures of Lebanon and Beirut all over the place. I am staring at pictures of the famous Raouche rock, our lady of Lebanon, the breathtaking mountain and sea view of Beirut from Harissa, the downtown martyr square of Beirut, our old generations in their cultural clothing, and our dabke dancers.

As I mesmerize these pictures of my Beirut, my mind can't stop listening to the Lebanese famous singer Fayrouz in the background singing "Ya Beirut". Everything felt surreal as if I was back home all over again. The pictures, the music, the atmosphere, and especially the food. Have you met anyone who does not adore Lebanese food? I am proud to be part of the garlic and onion stereotypes actually. Who wouldn't want to wake up in a city and smell the hummus?
But Beirut to me is not just the food, the music and places, it is also the language and its crazy outgoing people. As a traveler, I have been to countries where I did not feel the people were that friendly nor full of life as

the Lebanese people. One cultural shock that I had was when I was abroad working and realized as soon as I entered the office that it was dead. Everyone was quiet, keeping to themselves, no one greeted anyone, you basically just do your own thing and leave. I refused to be part of that and complained that "I am Lebanese, we greet and love to talk to one another at work and wherever we are, we can't stand silence".

Beirut to me is like the spirit of the Phoenix, destroyed and rebuilt 7 times as they say. As Majida Roumi once sang "Beirut, lady of the world, got up from under the ruins like a pine flower in April".

Beirut to me, is the Cedar of God trees among the snowy white mountains with a landscape of the Mediterranean blue sea less than an hour away. Beirut is the Sunday family gatherings and the importance of family and what our ancestors left behind. Beirut is where the brave women, men and children live and those who refuse to let the memories of war come between their joy of life. Beirut is the city of writings where the first law school was created. No wonder more than %90 of its citizens are literate.

Dear Beirut, I search for you in every city that I set foot on only to find you in its hidden places whispering to me to crawl back to you

Beirut, I love you

Biography

Rayan Ezzeddine born in 1994 is a young Lebanese Zimbabwean who is passionate about writing, travelling, exploring and learning. She obtained a Bachelor's degree in Political Science and International Affairs from the Lebanese American University in Beirut, Lebanon as well as a Master's degree in International Law and Human Rights from the University for Peace in San Jose, Costa Rica. Her passion for writing started around the age of 13 and she has continued to write since then. She considers herself a global citizen and a humanitarian traveler trying to give as much as she can to this temporary world. She hopes to inspire the youth with her writings to understand the reality of our world and to express their voices about it. She believes that the youth are the future of the world, the leaders, the activists and the change makers.

www.ingramcontent.com/pod-product-compliance
Ingram Content Group UK Ltd.
Pitfield, Milton Keynes, MK11 3LW, UK
UKHW040559210726
13854UKWH00008B/1547

9 781387 724024